Cacao Culture in the Philippines

The Tropical Climate, Plantation, Harvest and Economics of Cultivating the Cacao Plant

By William Scrugham Lyon

PANTIANOS
CLASSICS

Published by Pantianos Classics

ISBN-13: 978-1-78987-019-0

First published in Manila in 1902

Contents

Letter of Transmittal

Sir: I submit herewith an essay on the cultivation of cacao, for the use of planters in the Philippines. This essay is prompted first, because much of the cacao grown here is of such excellent quality as to induce keen rivalry among buyers to procure it at an advance of quite 50 per cent over the common export grades of the Java bean, notwithstanding the failure on the part of the local grower to "process" or cure the product in any way; second, because in parts of Mindanao and Negros, despite ill treatment or no treatment, the plant exhibits a luxuriance of growth and wealth of productiveness that demonstrates its entire fitness for those regions and leads us to believe in the successful extension of its propagation throughout these Islands; and lastly because of the repeated calls upon the Chief of the Agricultural Bureau for literature or information bearing upon this important horticultural industry.

The importance of cacao-growing in the Philippines can hardly be overestimated. Recent statistics place the world's demand for cacao (exclusive of local consumption) at 200,000,000 pounds, valued at more than $30,000,000 gold.

There is little danger of overproduction and consequent low prices for very many years to come. So far as known, the areas where cacao prospers in the great equatorial zone are small, and the opening and development of suitable regions has altogether failed to keep pace with the demand.

The bibliography of cacao is rather limited, and some of the best publications, [1] being in French, are unavailable to many. The leading English treatise, by Professor Hart, [2] admirable in many respects, deals mainly with conditions in Trinidad, West Indies, and is fatally defective, if not misleading, on the all-important question of pruning.

The life history of the cacao, its botany, chemistry, and statistics are replete with interest, and will, perhaps, be treated in a future paper.
Respectfully,

Wm. S. Lyon,
In Charge of Seed and Plant Introduction.
Hon. F. Lamson-Scribner,
Chief of the Insular Bureau of Agriculture.

[1] Le Cacaoyer, par Henri Jumelle. Culture de Cacaoyer dans Guadaloupe par Dr Paul Guerin.
[2] Cacao, by J. H. Hart, F. L. S. Trinidad.

Introduction

Cacao in cultivation exists nearly everywhere in the Archipelago. I have observed it in several provinces of Luzon, in Mindanao, Joló, Basilan, Panay, and Negros, and have well-verified assurances of its presence in Cebú, Bohol, and Masbate, and it is altogether reasonable to predicate its existence upon all the larger islands anywhere under an elevation of 1,000 or possibly 1,200 meters. Nevertheless, in many localities the condition of the plants is such as not to justify the general extension of cacao cultivation into all regions. The presence of cacao in a given locality is an interesting fact, furnishing a useful guide for investigation and agricultural experimentation, but, as the purpose of this paper is to deal with cacao growing from a commercial standpoint, it is well to state that wherever reference is made to the growth, requirements, habits, or cultural treatment of the plant the commercial aspect is alone considered. As an illustration, attention is called to the statement made elsewhere, that "cacao exacts a minimum temperature of 18°"; although, as is perfectly well known to the writer, its fruit has sometimes matured where the recorded temperatures have fallen as low as 10°. There is much to be learned here by experimentation, for as yet the cultivation is primitive in the extreme, pruning of any kind rudimentary or negative, and "treatment" of the nut altogether unknown.

Elsewhere in cacao-producing countries its cultivation has long passed the experimental stage, and the practices that govern the management of a well-ordered cacao plantation are as clearly defined as those of an orange grove in Florida or a vineyard in California.

In widely scattered localities the close observer will find many young trees that in vigor, color, and general health leave nothing to be desired, but before making final selection for a plantation he should inspect trees of larger growth for evidences of "die back" of the branches. If "die back" is present, superficial examination will generally determine if it is caused by neglect or by the attacks of insects. If not caused by neglect or insect attacks, he may assume that some primary essential to the continued and successful cultivation of the tree is wanting and that the location is unsuited to profitable plantations.

With due regard to these preliminary precautions and a close oversight of every subsequent operation, there is no reason why the growing of cacao may not ultimately become one of the most profitable horticultural enterprises that can engage the attention of planters in this Archipelago.

Climate

It is customary, when writing of any crop culture, to give precedence to site and soil, but in the case of cacao these considerations are of secondary importance, and while none of the minor operations of planting, pruning, cultivation, and fertilizing may be overlooked, they are all outweighed by the single essential—climate.

In general, a state of atmospheric saturation keeps pace with heavy rainfall, and for that reason we may successfully look for the highest relative humidity upon the eastern shores of the Archipelago, where the rainfall is more uniformly distributed over the whole year, than upon the west.

There are places where the conditions are so peculiar as to challenge especial inquiry. We find on the peninsula of Zamboanga a recorded annual mean rainfall of only 888 mm., and yet cacao (unirrigated) exhibits exceptional thrift and vigor. It is true that this rain is so evenly distributed throughout the year that every drop becomes available, yet the total rainfall is insufficient to account for the very evident and abundant atmospheric humidity indicated by the prosperous conditions of the cacao plantations. The explanation of this phenomenon, as made to me by the Rev. Father Algué, of the Observatory of Manila, is to the effect that strong equatorial ocean currents constantly prevail against southern Mindanao, and that their influence extend north nearly to the tenth degree of latitude. These currents, carrying their moisture-laden atmosphere, would naturally affect the whole of this narrow neck of land and influence as well some of the western coast of Mindanao, and probably place it upon the same favored hygrometric plane as the eastern coast, where the rainfall in some localities amounts to 4 meters a year.

While 2,000 mm. of mean annual rainfall equably distributed is ample to achieve complete success, it seems almost impossible to injure cacao by excessive precipitation. It has been known to successfully tide over inundation of the whole stem up to the first branches for a period covering nearly a month.

Irrigation must be resorted to in cases of deficient or unevenly distributed rainfall, and irrigation is always advantageous whenever there is suspension of rain for a period of more than fifteen days.

Concerning temperatures the best is that with an annual mean of 26° to 28°, with 20° as the mean minimum where any measure of success may be expected. A mean temperature of over 30° is prejudicial to cacao growing.

The last but not least important of the atmospheric phenomena for our consideration are the winds. Cacao loves to "steam and swelter in its own atmosphere" and high winds are inimical, and even refreshing breezes are incompatible, with the greatest success. As there are but few large areas in these Islands that are exempt from one or other of our prevailing winds, the remedies that suggest themselves are: The selection of small sheltered valleys where the prevailing winds are directly cut off by intervening hills or mountains; the plantation of only small groves in the open, and their frequent intersection by the plantation of rapid growing trees; and, best of all, plantings made in forest clearings, where the remaining forested lands will furnish the needed protection.

Location

It is always desirable to select a site that is approximately level or with only enough fall to assure easy drainage. Such sites may be planted symmetrically and are susceptible to the easiest and most economical application of the many operations connected with a plantation.

Provided the region is well forested and therefore protected from sea breezes, the plantation may be carried very near to the coast, provided the elevation is sufficient to assure the grove immunity from incursions of tide water, which, however much diluted, will speedily cause the death of the plants.

Excavations should be made during the dry season to determine that water does not stand within 1½ meters of the surface, a more essential condition, however, when planting is made "at stake" than when nursery reared trees are planted.

Hillsides, when not too precipitous, frequently offer admirable shelter and desirable soils, but their use entails a rather more complicated system of drainage, to carry away storm water without land washing, and for the ready conversion of the same into irrigating ditches during the dry season. Further, every operation involved must be performed by hand labor, and in the selection of such a site the planter must be largely influenced by the quantity and cost of available labor.

The unexceptionable shelter, the humidity that prevails, and the inexhaustible supply of humus that is generally found in deep forest ravines frequently lead to their planting to cacao where the slope is even as great as 45°. Such plantations, if done upon a considerable commercial scale, involve engineering problems and the careful terracing of each tree, and, except for a dearth of more suitable locations, is a practice that has little to commend it to the practical grower.

The Soil

Other things being equal, preference should be given to a not too tenacious, clayey loam. Selection, in fact, may be quite successfully made through the process of exclusion, and by eliminating all soils of a very light and sandy nature, or clays so tenacious that the surface bakes and cracks while still too wet within 3 or 4 inches of the surface to operate with farm tools. These excluded, still leave a very wide range of silt, clay, and loam soils, most of which are suitable to cacao culture.

Where properly protected from the wind a rocky soil, otherwise good, is not objectionable; in fact, such lands have the advantage of promoting good drainage.

Preparation of the Soil

When the plantation is made upon forest lands, it is necessary to cut and burn all underbrush, together with all timber trees other than those designed for shade. If such shade trees are left (and the advisability of leaving them will be discussed in the proper place), only those of the pulse or bean family are to be recommended. It should also be remembered that, owing in part to the close planting of cacao and in part to the fragility of its wood and its great susceptibility to damage resulting from wounds, subsequent removal of large shade trees from the plantation is attended with difficulty and expense, and the planter should leave few shade trees to the hectare. Clearing the land should be done during the dry season, and refuse burned in situ, thereby conserving to the soil the potash salts so essential to the continued well-being of cacao.

The land should be deeply plowed, and, if possible, subsoiled as well, and then, pending the time of planting the orchard, it may be laid down to corn, cotton, beans, or some forage plant. Preference should be given to "hoed crops," as it is essential to keep the surface in open tilth, as well as to destroy all weeds.

The common practice in most cacao-growing countries is to simply dig deep holes where the trees are to stand, and to give a light working to the rest of the surface just sufficient to produce the intermediate crops. This custom is permissible only on slopes too steep for the successful operation of a side hill plow, or where from lack of draft animals all cultivation has to be done by hand.

Cacao roots deeply, and with relatively few superficial feeders, and the deeper the soil is worked the better.

Drainage

The number and size of the drains will depend upon the amount of rainfall, the contour of the land, and the natural absorbent character of the soil. In no case should the ditches be less than 1 meter wide and 60 cm. deep, and if loose stones are at hand the sloping sides may be laid with them, which will materially protect them from washing by torrential rains.

These main drains should all be completed prior to planting. Connecting laterals may be opened subsequently, as the necessities of further drainage or future irrigation may demand; shallow furrows will generally answer for these laterals, and as their obliteration will practically follow every time cultivation is given, their construction may be of the cheapest and most temporary nature. Owing to the necessity of main drainage canals and the needful interplanting of shade plants between the rows of cacao, nothing is gained by laying off the land for planting in what is called "two ways," and all subsequent working of the orchard will consequently be in one direction.

The Plantation

Cacao, relatively to the size of the tree, may be planted very closely. We have stated that it rejoices in a close, moisture-laden atmosphere, and this permits of a closer planting than would be admissible with any other orchard crop.

In very rich soil the strong-growing Forastero variety may be planted 3.7 meters apart each way, or 745 trees to the hectare, and on lighter lands this, or the more dwarf-growing forms of Criollo, may be set as close as 3 meters or rather more than 1,000 trees to the hectare.

The rows should be very carefully lined out in one direction and staked where the young plants are to be set, and then (a year before the final planting) between each row of cacao a line of temporary shelter plants are to be planted. These should be planted in quincunx order, i. e., at the intersecting point of two lines drawn between the diagonal corners of the square made by four cacaos set equidistant each way. This temporary shelter is indispensable for the protection of the young plantation from wind and sun.

The almost universal custom is to plant, for temporary shelter, suckers of fruiting bananas, but throughout the Visayas and in Southern Luzon I think abacá could be advantageously substituted. It is true that, as commonly grown, abacá does not make so rank a growth as some of the plantains, but if given the perfect tillage which the cacao plantation should receive, and moderately rich soils, abacá ought to furnish all necessary shade. This temporary shade may be maintained till the fourth or fifth year, when it is to be grubbed out and the stalks and stumps, which are rich in nitrogen, may be left to decay upon the ground. At present prices, the four or five crops which may be secured from the temporary shelter plants ought to meet the expenses of the entire plantation until it comes into bearing.

In the next step, every fourth tree in the fourth or fifth row of cacao may be omitted and its place filled by a permanent shade tree. The planting of shade trees or "madre de cacao" among the cacao has been observed from time immemorial in all countries where the crop is grown, and the primary purpose of the planting has been for shade alone. Observing that these trees were almost invariably of the pulse or legume family, the writer, in the year 1892, raised the question, in the Proceedings of the Southern California Horticultural Society, that the probable benefits derived were directly attributable to the abundant fertilizing microörganisms developed in the soil by these leguminous plants, rather than the mechanical protection they afforded from the sun's rays.

To Mr. O. F. Cook, of the United States Department of Agriculture, however, belongs the credit of publishing, in 1901, [1] a résumé of his inquiries into the subject of the shades used for both the coffee and the cacao, and which fully confirmed the previous opinions that the main benefit derived from these trees was their influence in maintaining a constant supply of available nitrogen in the soil.

That cacao and its wild congenors naturally seek the shelter of well-shaded forests is well established; but having seen trees in these Islands that were fully exposed at all times showing no evidences of either scald, burn, or sun spot, and in every respect the embodiment of vigor and health, we are fully justified in assuming that here the climatic conditions are such as will permit of taking some reasonable liberties with this time-honored practice and supply needed nitrogen to the soil by the use of cheap and effective "catch crops," such us cowpeas or soy beans.

Here, as elsewhere, an Erythrina, known as "dap-dap," is a favorite shade tree among native planters; the rain tree (Pithecolobium saman) is also occasionally used, and in one instance only have I seen a departure from the use of the Leguminosæ, and that in western Mindanao, there is a shade plantation composed exclusively of Cananga odorata, locally known as ilang-ilang.

While not yet prepared to advocate the total exclusion of all shade trees, I am prepared to recommend a shade tree, if shade trees there must be, whose utility and unquestioned value has singularly escaped notice. The tree in question, the Royal Poinciana (Poinciana regia), embodies all of the virtues that are ascribed to the best of the pulse family, is easily procured, grows freely and rapidly from seed or cutting, furnishes a minimum of shade at all times, and, in these Islands, becomes almost leafless, at the season of maturity of the largest cacao crop when the greatest sun exposure is desired.

The remaining preparatory work consists in the planting of intersecting wind breaks at intervals throughout the grove, and upon sides exposed to winds, or where a natural forest growth does not furnish such a shelter belt. Unless the plantation lies in a particularly protected valley, no plantation, however large in the aggregate, should cover more than 4 or 5 hectares unbroken by at least one row of wind-break trees. Nothing that I know of can approach the mango for this purpose. It will hold in check the fiercest gale and give assurance to the grower that after any storm his cacao crop is still on the trees and not on the ground, a prey to ants, mice, and other vermin.

[1] "Shade in Coffee Culture." U. S. Dept. Ag., Washington, 1901.

Selection of Varieties

All the varieties of cacao in general cultivation may be referred to three general types, the Criollo, Forastero, and Calabacillo; and of these, those that I have met in cultivation in the Archipelago are the first and second only. The Criollo is incomparably the finest variety in general use, and may perhaps be most readily distinguished by the inexperienced through the ripe but unfermented seed or almond, as it is often called. This, on breaking, is found to be whitish or yellowish-white, while the seeds of those in which the Forastero or Calabacillo blood predominates are reddish, or, in the case of Forastero, almost violet in color. For flavor, freedom from bitterness, facility in curing, and high commercial value, the Criollo is everywhere conceded to be *facile princeps.*

On the other hand, in point of yield, vigor, freedom from disease, and compatibility to environment it is not to be compared with the others. Nevertheless, where such perfect conditions exist as are found in parts of Mindanao, I do not hesitate to urge the planting of Criollo. Elsewhere, or wherever the plantation is tentative or the conditions not very well known to the planter, the Forastero is to be recommended. The former is commercially known as *"Caracas"* and *"old red Ceylon,"* and may be obtained from Ceylon dealers; and the latter, the Forastero, or forms of it which have originated in the island, can be procured from Java.

intact to the field. Plants thus reared give to the inexperienced an assurance of success not always obtained by the trained or veteran planter of bare rooted subjects.

Cultivation

Planters are united in the opinion that pruning, cutting, or in any way lacerating the roots is injurious to the cacao, and in deference to this opinion all cultivation close to the tree should be done with a harrow-tooth cultivator, or shallow scarifier. All intermediate cultivation should be deep and thorough, whenever the mechanical condition of the soil will permit it. A plant stunted in youth will never make a prolific tree; early and continuous growth can only be secured by deep and thorough cultivation.

Of even more consideration than an occasional root cutting is any injury, however small, to the tree stem, and on this account every precaution should be taken to protect the trees from accidental injury when plowing or cultivating. The whiffletree of the plow or cultivator used should be carefully fendered with rubber or a soft woolen packing that will effectually guard against the carelessness of workmen. Wounds in the bark or stem offer an inviting field for the entry of insects or the spores of fungi, and are, furthermore, apt to be overlooked until the injury becomes deep seated and sometimes beyond repair.

With the gradual extension of root development, cultivation will be reduced to a narrow strip between the rows once occupied by the plantain or the abacá, but, to the very last, the maintenance of the proper soil conditions should be observed by at least one good annual plowing and by as many superficial cultivations as the growth of the trees and the mechanical state of the land will admit.

Pruning

When left to its own resources the cacao will fruit for an almost indefinite time. When well and strenuously grown it will bear much more abundant fruit from its fifth to its twenty-fifth year, and by a simple process of renewal can be made productive for a much longer time.

A necessary factor to this result is an annual pruning upon strictly scientific lines. The underlying principle involved is, primarily, the fact that the cacao bears its crop directly upon the main branches and trunk, and not upon spurs or twigs; secondly, that wood under three years is rarely fruitful, and that only upon stems or branches of five years or upward does the maximum fruitfulness occur; that the seat of inflorescence is directly over the axil of a fallen leaf, from whence the flowers are born at irregular times throughout the year.

With this necessary, fundamental information as a basis of operations, the rational system of pruning that suggests itself is the maintenance of as large an extension at all times of straight, well-grown mature wood and the perfecting of that by the early and frequent removal of all limbs or branches that the form of the tree does not admit of carrying without overcrowding.

It is desirable that this extension of the branch system should be lateral rather than vertical, for the greater facility with which fruit may be plucked and possible insect enemies fought; and on this account the leading growths should be stopped when a convenient height has been attained.

When well grown and without accident to its leader, the cacao will naturally branch at from 1 to 1.4 meters from the ground. These primary branches are mostly three to five in number, and all in excess of three should be removed as soon as selection can be made of three strongest that are as nearly equidistant from each other as may be. When these branches are from 80 cm. to 1 meter long, and preferably the shorter distance, they are to be stopped by pinching the extremities. This will cause them and the main stem as well to "break," i. e., to branch in many places.

At this point the vigilance and judgment of the planter are called into greater play. These secondary branches are, in turn, all to be reduced as were the primary ones, and their selection can not be made in a symmetrical whorl, for the habit of the tree does not admit of it, and selection of the three should be made with reference to their future extension, that the interior of the tree should not be overcrowded and that such outer branches be retained as shall fairly maintain the equilibrium of the crown.

This will complete the third year and the formative stage of the plant. Subsequent prunings will be conducted on the same lines, with the modification that when the secondary branches are again cut back, the room in the head of the tree will rarely admit of more than one, at most two, tertiary branches being allowed to remain. When these are grown to an extent that brings the total height of the tree to 3 or 4 meters, they should be cut back annually, at the close of the dry season. Such minor operations as the removal of thin, wiry, or hide-bound growths and all suckers suggest themselves to every horticulturist, whether he be experienced in cacao growing or not. When a tree is exhausted by over-bearing, or has originally been so ill formed that it is not productive, a strong sucker or "gourmand" springing from near the ground may be encouraged to grow. By distributing the pruning over two or three periods, in one year the old tree can be entirely removed and its place substituted by the "gourmand." During the third year flowers will be abundant and some fruit will set, but it is advisable to remove it while small and permit all of the energy of the plant to be expended in wood making.

Plate 1.—Shows the interesting, fruit bearing habit of the Cacao.

From what we know of its flowering habit, it is obvious that every operation connected with the handling or pruning of a cacao, should be conducted with extreme care; to see that the bark is never injured about the old leaf scars, for to just the extent it is so injured is the fruit-bearing area curtailed. Further, no pruning cut should ever be inflicted, except with the sharpest of knives and saws, and the use of shears, that always bruise to some extent, is to be

19

avoided. All the rules that are laid down for the guidance of the pruning of most orchard trees in regard to clean cuts, sloping cuts, and the covering of large wounds with tar or resin apply with fourfold force to the cacao. Its wood is remarkably spongy and an easy prey to the enemies ever lying in wait to attack it, and the surest remedies for disease are preventive ones, and by the maintenance of the bark of the tree at all times in the sound condition, we are assured that it is best qualified to resist invasion. Of the great number of worm-riddled trees to be seen in the Archipelago, it is easy in every case to trace the cause to the neglect and brutal treatment which left them in a condition to invite the attacks of disease of every kind.

Harvest

The ripening period of cacao generally occurs at two seasons of the year, but in these islands the most abundant crop is obtained at about the commencement of the dry season, and the fruits continue to ripen for two months or longer. The time of its approaching maturity is easily recognized by the tyro by the unmistakable aroma of chocolate that pervades the orchard at that period, and by some of the pods turning reddish or yellow according to the variety.

The pods are attached by a very short stalk to the trunk of the tree, and those within reach of the hand are carefully cut with shears. Those higher up are most safely removed with an extension American tree pruner. A West Indian hook knife with a cutting edge above and below and mounted on a bamboo pole, if kept with the edges very sharp, does excellently well, but should only be intrusted to the most careful workmen. There is hardly a conceivable contingency to warrant the climbing of a cacao tree. If it should occur, the person climbing should go barefooted. As soon as the fruit, or so much of it as is well ripened, has been gathered, it is thrown into heaps and should be opened within twenty-four hours.

The opening is done in a variety of ways, but the practice followed in Surinam would be an excellent one here if experienced labor was not at command. There, with a heavy knife or cutlass (bolo), they cut off the base or stem end of the fruit and thereby expose the column to which the seeds are attached, and then women and children, who free most of the seeds, are able to draw out the entire seed mass intact. It is exceedingly important that the seeds are not wounded, and for that reason it is inexpedient to intrust the more expeditious method of halving the fruit with a sharp knife to any but experienced workmen.

The process of curing that I have seen followed in these Islands is simplicity itself. Two jars half filled with water are provided for the cleaners, and as the seeds are detached from the pulp they are sorted and graded on the spot. Only those of large, uniform size, well formed and thoroughly ripe, being thrown into one; deformed, small, and imperfectly matured seeds going to the other. In these jars the seeds are allowed to stand in their own juice for a day, then they are taken out, washed in fresh water, dried in the sun from two to four days, according to the weather, and the process from the Filipino standpoint is complete.

Much of the product thus obtained is singularly free from bitterness and of such excellent quality; as to be saleable at unusually high prices, and at the same time in such good demand that it is with some hesitancy that the process of fermentation is recommended for general use.

But it is also equally certain that localities in these Islands will be planted to cacao where all the conditions that help to turn out an unrivaled natural product are by no means assured. For such places, where the rank-growing, more coarse-flavored, and bitter-fruited Forastero may produce exceptionally good crops, it will become incumbent on the planter to adopt some of the many methods of fermentation, whereby he can correct the crudeness of the untreated bean and receive a remunerative price for the "processed" or ameliorated product.

Undoubtedly the Strickland method, or some modification of it, is the best, and is now in general use on all considerable estates where the harvest is 200 piculs or upward per annum, and its use probably assures a more uniform product than any of the ruder processes in common use by small proprietors.

But it must not be forgotten that the present planters in the Philippines are all small proprietors, and that until such time as the maturing of large plantations calls for the more elaborate apparatus of the Strickland pattern, some practice whereby the inferior crude bean may be economically and quickly converted into a marketable product can not be avoided. As simple and efficacious as any is that largely pursued in some parts of Venezuela, where is produced the famous Caracas cacao.

The beans and pulp are thrown into wooden vats that are pierced with holes sufficient to permit of the escape of the juice, for which twenty-four hours suffices. The vat is then exposed to the sun for five or six hours, and the beans, while still hot, are taken out, thrown into large heaps, and covered with blankets.

The next day they are returned to the box, subjected to a strong sun heat and again returned to the heap. This operation is repeated for several days, until the beans, by their bright chocolate color and suppleness, indicate that they are cured. If, during the period of fermentation, rain is threatened or occurs, the beans are shoveled, still hot, into bags and retained there until they can once more be exposed to the sun. Before the final bagging they are carefully hand rubbed in order to remove the adherent gums and fibrous matters that did not pass off in the primary fermentation.

In Ceylon, immediately after the beans have been fermented they are washed, and the universally high prices obtained by the Ceylon planters make it desirable to reproduce here a brief résumé of their method. The fermentation is carried on under sheds, and the beans are heaped up in beds of 60 cm. to 1 meter in thickness upon a platform of parallel joists arranged to permit of the escape of the juices. This platform is elevated from the ground and the whole heap is covered with sacks or matting. The fermentation takes from five to seven days, according to the heat of the atmosphere and the size of the heap, and whenever the temperature rises above 40° the mass is carefully turned over with wooden shovels.

Immediately after the fermentation is completed the Ceylon planter passes the mass through repeated washings, and nothing remains but to dry the seed. This in Ceylon is very extensively done, in dryers of different kinds, some patterned after the American fruit dryer, some in slowly rotating cylinders through the axis of which a powerful blast of hot air is driven.

The process of washing unquestionably diminishes somewhat the weight of the cured bean; for that reason the practice is not generally followed in other countries, but in the case of the Ceylon product it is one of the contributing factors to the high prices obtained.

Enemies and Diseases

Monkeys, rats, and parrots are here and in all tropical countries the subject of much complaint, and if the plantation is remote from towns or in the forest, their depredations can only be held in check by the constant presence of well-armed hunter or watchman. Of the more serious enemies with which we have to deal, pernicious insects and in particular those that attack the wood of the tree, everything has yet to be learned.

Mr. Charles N. Banks, an accomplished entomologist, now stationed at Maao, Occidental Negros, is making a close study of the life history of the insect enemies of cacao, and through his researches it is hoped that much light will be thrown upon the whole subject and that ways will be devised to overcome and prevent the depredations of these insect pests. The most formidable insect that has so far been encountered is a beetle, which pierces and deposits its eggs within the bark. When the worm hatches, it enters the wood and traverses it longitudinally until it is ready to assume the mature or beetle state, when it comes to the surface and makes its escape. These worms will frequently riddle an entire branch and even enter the trunk. The apertures that the beetle makes for the laying of its eggs are so small—more minute than the head of a pin—that discovery and probing for the worm with a fine wire is not as fruitful of results as has been claimed.

Of one thing, however, we are positively assured, i. e., that the epoch of ripening of the cacao fruit is the time when its powerful fragrance serves to attract the greatest number of these beetles and many other noxious insects to the grove. This, too, is the time when the most constant and abundant supply of labor is on the plantation and when vast numbers of these insects can be caught and destroyed. The building of small fires at night in the groves, as commonly practiced here and in many tropical countries, is attended with some benefits. Lately, in India, this remedy has been subject to an improvement that gives promise of results which will in time minimize the ravages of insect pests. It is in placing powerful acetylene lights over broad, shallow vats of water overlaid with mineral oil or petroleum. Some of these lamps now made under recent patents yield a light of dazzling brilliancy, and if well distributed would doubtless lure millions of insects to their death. The cheap cost of the fuel also makes the remedy available for trial by every planter.

There is a small hemipterous insect which stings the fruit when about two-thirds grown, and deposits its eggs within. For this class of insects M. A. Tonduz, who has issued publications on the diseases of cacao in Venezuela, recommends washing the fruit with salt water, and against the attacks of beetles in general by painting the tree stem and branches with Bordeaux mixture, or with the vassiliére insecticide, of which the basis is a combination of whale-oil soap and petroleum suspended in lime wash. There can be no possible virtue in the former, except as a preventive against possible fungous diseases; of the sanitive value of the latter we can also afford to be skeptical, as the mechanical sealing of the borer's holes, and thereby cutting off the air supply, would only result in driving the worm sooner to the surface. The odor of petroleum and particularly of whale-oil soap is so repellent, however, to most insects that its prophylactic virtues would undoubtedly be great.

The Philippine Islands appear to be so far singularly exempt from the very many cryptogamic or fungous diseases, blights, mildews, rusts, and cankers that have played havoc with cacao-growing in many countries. That we should enjoy continued immunity will depend greatly upon securing seeds or young plants only from non-infested districts or from reputable dealers, who will carefully disinfect any shipments, and to supplement this by a close microscopical examination upon arrival and the immediate burning of any suspected shipments.

Another general precaution that will be taken by every planter who aims to maintain the best condition in his orchard is the gathering and burning of all prunings or trimmings from the orchard, whether they are diseased or not. Decaying wood of any kind is a field for special activity for insect life and fungous growth, and the sooner it is destroyed the better.

On this account it is customary in some countries to remove the fruit pods from the field. But unless diseased, or unless they are to be returned after the harvest, they should be buried upon the land for their manurial value.

Manuring

There are few cultivated crops that make less drain upon soil fertility than cacao, and few drafts upon the land are so easily and inexpensively returned. From an examination made of detailed analyses by many authors and covering many regions, it may be broadly stated that an average crop of cacao in the most-favored districts is about 9 piculs per hectare, and that of the three all-important elements of nitrogen, phosphoric acid, and potash, a total of slightly more than 4.2 kilograms is removed in each picul of cured seeds harvested. These 37 kilos of plant food that are annually taken from each hectare may be roughly subdivided as follows:

18 kilos of nitrogen,

10 kilos of potash,

9 kilos of phosphoric acid.

On this basis, after the plantation is in full bearing, we would have to make good with standard fertilizers each year for each hectare about 220 kilos of nitrate of soda, or, if the plantation was shaded with leguminous trees, only one-half that amount, or 110 kilos. Of potash salts, say the sulphate, only one-half that amount, or 55 kilos, if the plantation was unshaded. If, however, it was shaded, as the leguminous trees are all heavy feeders of potash, we would have to double the amount and use 110 kilos.

In any case, as fixed nitrogen always represents a cost quite double that of potash, from an economical standpoint the planter is still the gainer who supplies potash to the shade trees. There still remains phosphoric acid, which, in the form of the best superphosphate of lime, would require 55 kilos for unshaded orchards, and about 70 if dap-dap, Pionciana, or any leguminous tree was grown in the orchard. These three ingredients may be thoroughly incorporated and used as a top dressing and lightly harrowed in about each tree.

If the commercial nitrates can not be readily obtained, then recourse must be had to the sparing use of farm manures. Until the bearing age these may be used freely, but after that with caution and discrimination. Although I have seen trees here that have been bearing continuously for twenty-two years, I have been unable to find so much as one that to the knowledge of the oldest resident has ever been fertilized in any way, yet, notwithstanding our lack of knowledge of local conditions, it seems perfectly safe to predicate that liberal manuring with stable manure or highly ammoniated fertilizers would insure a rank, succulent growth that is always prejudicial to the best and heaviest fruit production. In this I am opposed to Professor Hart, [1] who seems to think that stable manures are those only that may be used with a free hand.

We have many safe ways of applying nitrogen through the medium of various catch crops of pulse or beans, with the certainty that we can never overload the soil with more than the adjacent tree roots can take up and thoroughly assimilate. When the time comes that the orchard so shades the ground that crops can no longer be grown between the rows, then, in preference to stable manures I would recommend cotton-seed cake or "poonac," the latter being always obtainable in this Archipelago.

While the most desirable form in which potash can be applied is in the form of the sulphate, excellent results have been had with the use of Kainit or Stassfurth salts, and as a still more available substitute, wood ashes is suggested. When forest lands are near, the underbrush may be cut and burned in a clearing or wherever it may be done without detriment to the standing timber, and the ashes scattered in the orchard before they have been leached by rains. The remaining essential of phosphoric acid in the form of superphosphates will for some years to come necessarily be the subject of direct importation. In the cheap form of phosphate slag it is reported to have been used with great success in both Grenada and British Guiana, and would be well worthy of trial here.

Lands very rich in humus, as some of our forest valleys are, undoubtedly carry ample nitrogenous elements of fertility to maintain the trees at a high standard of growth for many years, but provision is indispensable for a regular supply of potash and phosphoric acid as soon as the trees come into heavy bearing. It is to them and not to the nitrogen that we look for the formation of strong, stocky, well-ripened wood capable of fruit bearing and for fruit that shall be sound, highly flavored, and well matured.

The bearing life of such a tree will surely be healthfully prolonged for many years beyond one constantly driven with highly stimulating foods, and in the end amply repay the grower for the vigilance, toil, and original expenditure of money necessary to maintaining a well-grown and well-appointed cacao plantation.

[1] "Cacao," p. 16.

Supplemental Notes

New Varieties.—Cacao is exclusively grown from seed, and it is only by careful selection of the most valuable trees that the planter can hope to make the most profitable renewals or additions to his plantations. It is by this means that many excellent sorts are now in cultivation in different regions that have continued to vary from the three original, common forms of Theobroma cacao, until now it is a matter of some difficulty to differentiate them.

Residence.—The conditions for living in the Philippines offer peculiar, it may be said unexampled, advantages to the planter of cacao. The climate as a whole is remarkably salubrious, and sites are to be found nearly everywhere for the estate buildings, sufficiently elevated to obviate the necessity of living near stagnant waters.

Malarial fevers are relatively few, predacious animals unknown, and insects and reptiles prejudicial to human life or health extraordinarily few in number. In contrast to this we need only call attention to the entire Caribbean coast of South America, where the climate and soil conditions are such that the cacao comes to a superlative degree of perfection, and yet the limits of its further extension have probably been reached by the insuperable barrier of a climate so insalubrious that the Caucasian's life is one endless conflict with disease, and when not engaged in active combat with some form of malarial poisoning his energies are concentrated upon battle with the various insect or animal pests that make life a burden in such regions.

Nonresidence upon a cacao plantation is an equivalent term for ultimate failure. Every operation demands the exercise of the observant eye and the directing hand of a master, but there is no field of horticultural effort that offers more assured reward, or that will more richly repay close study and the application of methods wrought out as the sequence of those studies.

Estimated Cost and Revenues Derived from a Cacao Plantation

Estimates of expenses in establishing a cacao farm in the Visayas and profits after the fifth year. The size of the farm selected is 16 hectares, the amount of land prescribed by Congress of a single public land entry. The cost of procuring such a tract of land is as yet undetermined and can not be reckoned in the following tables. The prices of the crop are estimated at 48 cents per kilo, which is the current price for the best grades of cacao in the world's markets. The yield per tree is given as 2 catties, or 1.25 kilos, a fair and conservative estimate for a good tree, with little or no cultivation. The prices for unskilled labor are 25 per cent in advance of the farm hand in the Visayan islands. No provision is made for management or supervision, as the owner will, it is assumed, act as manager.

Charges to capital account are given for the second, third, and fourth year, but no current expenses are given, for other crops are to defray operating expenses until the cacao trees begin to bear. No estimate of residence is given. All accounts are in United States currency.

Expendable the first year.

Capital account:

Clearing of average brush and timber land, at $15 per hectare $340.00	
Four carabaos, plows, harrows, cultivators, carts, etc.	550.00
Breaking and preparing land, at $5 per hectare	80.00
Opening main drainage canals, at $6 per hectare	96.00
Tool house and storeroom	200.00
Purchase and planting 10,000 abacá stools, at 2 cents each	200.00
Seed purchase, rearing and planting 12,000 cacao, at 3 cents each	360.00
Contingent and incidental	174.00
Total	$2,000.00

28

Interest on investment	$200.00
Depreciation on tools, buildings, and animals (20 per cent of cost)	
	150.00
	350.00

Third year.

Interest on investment	$200.00
Depreciation as above	150.00
	350.00

Fourth year.

Interest on investment	$200.00
Depreciation as above	150.00
Building of drying house and sweat boxes, capacity 20,000 kilos	
	450.00
	$800.00
Total capital investment	3,500.00

Fifth year.

Income account:
From 11,680 cacao trees, 300 grams cacao each, equals 3,500 kilos, at 48 cents   1,680.00

Expense account:
Fixed interest and depreciation charges on investment of	$3,500.00
	$350.00
Taxes 1½ per cent on a one-third valuation basis of $250 per hectare	
	60.00
Cultivating, pruning, etc., at $5.50 per hectare	88.00
Fertilizing, at $6 per hectare	96.00
Harvesting, curing, packing 3,500 kilos cacao, at 10 cents per kilo	
	350.00
Contingent	86.00

| | | 1,030.00 |
| Credit balance | | 650.00 |

Sixth year.

Income account:

From 11,680 cacao trees, at 500 grams cacao each, equals 5,840 kilos, at 48 cents — 2,803.20

Expense account:	
Fixed interest and depreciation charges as above	$350.00
Taxes as above	60.00
Cultivating, etc., as above	88.00
Fertilizing, at $8 per hectare	128.00
Harvesting, etc., 5,840 kilos cacao, at 10 cents per kilo	584.00
Contingent	93.20
	1,303.20
Credit balance	1,500.00

Seventh year.

Income account:

From 11,680 cacao trees, at 750 grams cacao each, equals 8,760 kilos, at 48 cents — 4,204.80

Expense account:	
Fixed interest charges as above	$350.00
Taxes as above	60.00
Cultivating, etc., as above	88.00
Fertilizing, at $10 per hectare	160.00
Harvest, etc., of 8,760 kilos of cacao, at 10 cents per kilo	876.00
Contingent	170.80
	1,704.80
Credit balance	2,500.00

Eighth year.

Income account:

From 11,680 cacao trees, at 1 kilo cacao each, equals 11,680 kilos, at
48 cents $5,606.40

Expense account:

Fixed interest charges as above	$350.00
Taxes as above	60.00
Cultivating, etc., as above	88.00
Fertilizing, at $12.50 per hectare	200.00
Harvest, etc., 11,680 kilos of cacao, at 10 cents per kilo	1,168.00
Contingent	240.40
	2,106.40
Credit balance	3,500.00

Ninth year.

Income account:

From 11,680 trees, at 2 "catties" or 1.25 kilos cacao each, equals
14,600 kilos, at 48 cents   7,008.00

Expense account:

Fixed interest charges as above	$350.00
Taxes at 1½ per cent on a one-third valuation of $500 per hectare	120.00
Cultivation and pruning as above	88.00
Fertilizing, at $15 per hectare	240.00
Harvesting, etc., of 14,600 kilos of cacao, at 10 cents per kilo	1,460.00
Contingent	250.00
	2,508.00
Credit balance	4,500.00

In the tenth year there should be no increase in taxes or fertilizers, and a slight increase in yield, sufficient to bring the net profits of the estate to the approximate amount of $5,000. This would amount to a dividend of rather more than $312 per hectare, or its equivalent of about $126 per acre.

These tables further show original capitalization cost of nearly $90 per acre, and from the ninth year annual operating expenses of rather more than $60 per acre.

It should be stated, however, that the operating expenses are based upon a systematic and scientific management of the estate; while the returns or income are based upon revenue from trees that are at the disadvantage of being without culture of any kind, and, while I am of the opinion that the original cost per acre of the plantation, nor its current operating expenses may be much reduced below the figures given, I feel that there is a reasonable certainty that the crop product may be materially increased beyond the limit of two "catties."

In Camerouns, Dr. Preuss, a close and well-trained observer, gives the mean annual yield of trees of full-bearing age at 4.4 pounds.

Mr. Rousselot places the yield on the French Congo at the same figure. In the Caroline Islands it reaches 5 pounds and in Surinam, according to M. Nichols, the average at maturity is 6½ pounds. In Mindanao, I have been told, but do not vouch for the report, of more than ten "catties" taken in one year from a single tree; and, as there are well-authenticated instances of record, of single trees having yielded as much as 30 pounds, I am not prepared to altogether discredit the Mindanao story.

The difference, however, between good returns and enormous profits arising from cacao growing in the Philippines will be determined by the amount of knowledge, experience, and energy that the planter is capable of bringing to bear upon the culture in question.